SEEDS Pop·Stick·Glide

SEEDS Pop · Stick · Glide

TEXT BY *Patricia Lauber* PHOTOGRAPHS BY *Jerome Wexler*

Crown Publishers, Inc., New York

PHOTO CREDITS

A. W. Ambler/Photo Researchers, 46; Lynwood M. Chace/Photo Researchers, 47 (top); Richard Dranitzke/ Photo Researchers, 39 (right); Carl Frank/Photo Researchers, 39 (left); Dr. Wm. M. Harlow/Photo Researchers, 23 (top); Tom McHugh/Photo Researchers, 36; Charles E. Mohr/Photo Researchers, 47 (bottom); Leonard Lee Rue III, 37; Ruth M. Smiley/Photo Researchers, 38.

Text copyright © 1981 by Patricia Lauber
Photographs copyright © 1981 by Jerome Wexler

10 9 8 7 6 5 4 3 2 1

The text of this book is set in 12 point Century Schoolbook.
The illustrations are black-and-white photographs.

Library of Congress Cataloging in Publication Data

Lauber, Patricia.   Seeds, pop! stick! glide!   Summary: Text and photographs describe the many different ways that seeds travel and disperse. 1. Seeds—Dispersal—Juvenile literature. [1. Seeds—Dispersal]
I. Wexler, Jerome. II. Title.   QK929.L38   582′.0467   80-14553   ISBN 0-517-54165-3

Contents

Plants on the Move

Most flowering plants are rooted in the ground. They cannot run, fly, swim, or crawl. Yet many kinds do have a way of traveling. You see the proof every spring. Last year there were no thistles in that empty lot next door. This year there are. Your vegetable patch has young dandelions, plantain, and other things you did not plant. A few yards from a big maple tree you find a tiny maple seedling.

Where did all these plants come from? They grew from seeds that traveled away from the parent plants. The parent plants stayed in place, but their flowers made seeds that traveled.

Flowers have many sizes, shapes, and colors, but they are alike in what they do. They make seeds, which give rise to new plants.

Seeds form inside a flower. As they start to ripen, the flower petals fade and wither away. Other parts of the flower also dry up and fall off. But one part is still growing. This is the part that holds the seeds. It is called a fruit. Some fruits are kinds you eat—cherries, peaches, melons, blueberries—but most are not. Fruits are simply the plant parts that hold the seeds. Some seeds travel in their fruits. Others travel alone.

Most flowering plants make many seeds. If they all fell to the ground around the parent plant, there would be no room for the young plants to grow. But this does not happen if the seeds travel. At least some of them will reach places where new plants can grow.

How do seeds travel? In this book you will discover some of the many and wonderful ways in which seeds get about.

Travelers with Animals and People

STICKTIGHT

You have been for a fall walk. Home again, you find you are covered with sticktights. They came from a plant you brushed against. Probably you didn't even see it. It grows almost everywhere, but it is easy to miss. That's a sticktight plant in the lower right-hand corner of the photograph.

The sticktight is a plant with seeds that travel on people and animals.

You pull the sticktights off and throw them away. If you do this out-doors, you are giving the seeds a chance to sprout and grow.

The seeds were made by the flowers. A sticktight plant has tiny yellow-orange flowers. They grow in groups, or clusters. A cluster of tiny flowers is called a flower head. This photograph shows two sticktight flower heads, each about the size of a bee. By fall the petals have dropped off the flowers, and sticktights have formed.

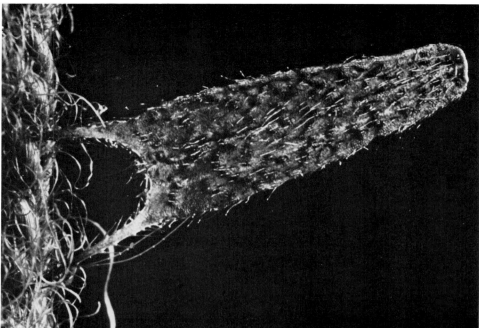

Sticktights are small. They look like seeds, but they are really fruits. Each sticktight holds one seed. When you brush against a sticktight the points and barbs hook your clothing. You carry off the sticktight and its seeds.

Animals carry away sticktights in their fur and feathers. Later they may pull the sticktights off and drop them on the ground. Or a sticktight may rub off against a rock or bush.

If a sticktight falls in a good place for growing, the seed inside will sprout and a new plant will spring up. The tiny plant at right has put down roots. Now it is pushing off the fruit that held the seed. If nothing harms it, it will grow into a big sticktight plant, with its own flowers and fruits and seeds.

4

GREAT BURDOCK

Here's another plant whose seeds travel with animals and people. Its name is great burdock. It, too, grows almost everywhere—in fields, in empty city lots, beside roads, on the edge of woods, and even in gardens.

Great burdock blooms in summer and early fall. Its tiny pink-purple flowers grow in flower heads. These flower heads are just opening.

Do you see some little hooks? These are leaf-like parts that are called bracts. Burdock bracts surround the flower head. They are something like a cage. At first they are soft.

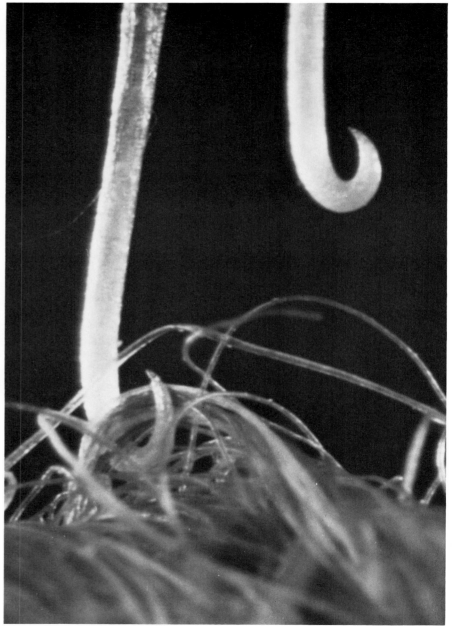

As time passes, the flowers form fruits and seeds. The seeds ripen. By then the bracts are as stiff and sharp as fishhooks. The flower head has become a burr. The photograph at right shows what happens if you brush against one.

A burdock burr is hard to get rid of. Pick it off your clothes and it sticks to your fingers. The hooks become tangled in animal fur and do not work loose. Even so, its seeds are spread by animals and people.

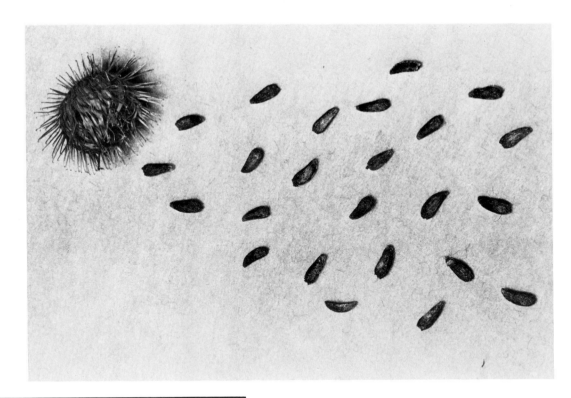

As a burr is carried away, the fruits are shaken out of the cage of bracts. Some fall in places where their seeds can sprout and grow.

The burrs also stick to one another. You can use them to make something—a basket, an animal, a tree.

QUEEN ANNE'S LACE

This plant has many small white flowers. They form flower heads that look like white lace. Its name is Queen Anne's lace.

Some flower heads are rounded, and some are flat. Each has the shape of an umbrella. The stem is the handle. The flower stalks are the umbrella ribs.

Queen Anne's lace is easy to find in summer. It grows in many places.

Look for it again in late fall or early winter, after a hard frost. Now the plant is dead. Its white petals are gone, but you can see the fruits. They are attached to the ribs of the umbrella.

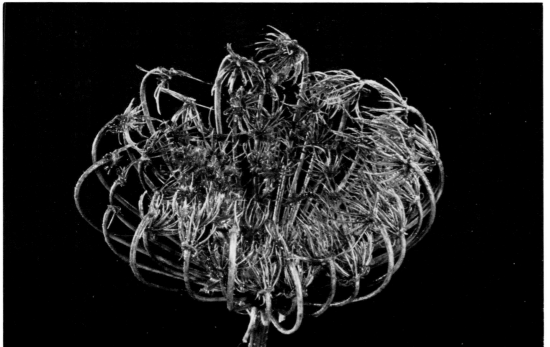

On a sunny day, gently pick an umbrella and take it home. Put it head down in a pail of water and watch what happens. In ten to fifteen minutes the wet umbrella will close up into a ball, like a bird's nest.

9

Then put the umbrella in a glass without water. If the air is dry, the ball will open up in a few hours. If the air is damp, the ball may take a few days to open.

You can see the same changes take place outdoors. The umbrellas are open in dry weather. They close up on rainy days. The opening and closing play a part in spreading the fruits and their seeds.

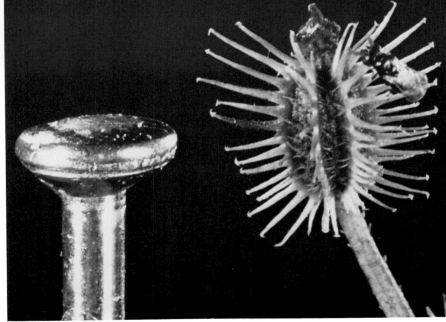

The fruits grow in pairs, which break apart when they are fully ripe. Each pair is about the size of a pinhead. The fruits are hard and ribbed. Along each rib is a row of hairs.

The hairs will stick to animal fur that is dry, but they cannot stick to fur that is wet and slippery.

Suppose an animal brushes against a plant on a wet day. If the umbrella were open, the fruits would fall to the ground under the parent plant. But this does not happen because on wet days the umbrella is closed up, with its fruits inside. It is open only in dry weather, when its fruits will stick to fur and be carried away.

BROAD-LEAVED PLANTAIN

For other plants, a wet day may help to spread the seeds. Some fruits and seeds become sticky when wet. They may stick to people and animals, and to dead leaves that the wind will carry away. Broad-leaved plantain is one of these plants. You find it growing in lawns and gardens and driveways, as well as in city lots and along the sides of roads.

When the plantain was in bloom, tiny flowers covered its tall stalks. Each flower formed a fruit (right), holding two or more seeds. When the seeds are ripe, the fruit opens around the middle. The seeds are small and light. On a dry windy day they may blow away.

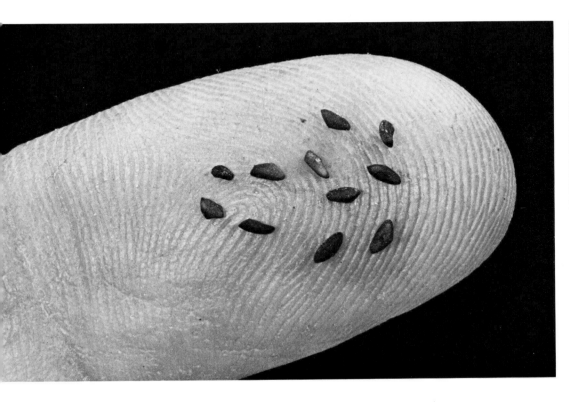

On a rainy day a seed that becomes wet gives off a sticky jelly. You can see the jelly case around this seed, which is on a toothpick. Jelly-covered seeds stick to animals, leaves, and people's shoes, socks, and pant legs.

FLOWERING DOGWOOD

The flowering dogwood also makes seeds that travel with animals. But these seeds do not stick to fur, feathers, or feet. They are eaten, and so they travel inside animals.

  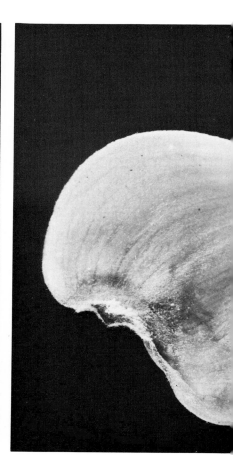

In bloom a dogwood seems to have big pink or white petals, but these are not really petals. They are bracts—leaf-like parts. The flowers, as you can see, are clustered at the center of the bracts. They are tiny.

The fruits that form are round, bright red, and fleshy. Inside each fruit is a single seed. Here, part of a fruit has been cut away to show the seed (below).

The fruits and their seeds are eaten by many animals—birds, skunks, deer, rabbits, squirrels. Some of the seeds are chewed up or crushed. Nothing will grow from them. Others may be spit out, or they may pass through the animal and fall to earth in its droppings. That is how the seeds are spread.

Many, many kinds of fruits are food for animals. Plants make the food, and animals spread the plants' seeds.

PIN OAK

Do oak trees have flowers? It may surprise you, but they do. They too have flowers that make fruits and seeds. The oak's fruit is an acorn. The seed is the nut meat inside.

There are two big groups of oaks—red oaks and white oaks. This tree is one of the red oaks. It is the kind called a pin oak.

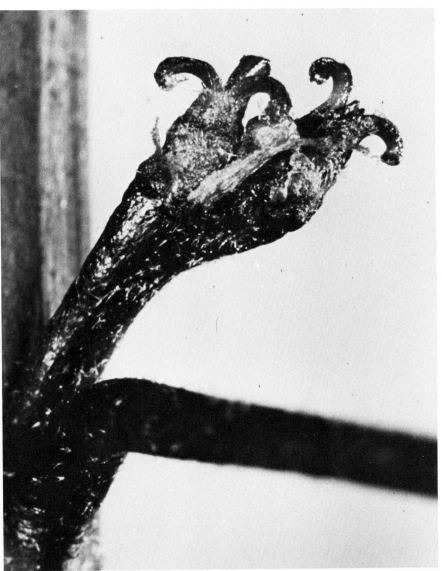

Here is the little red flower that becomes the fruit. It's the size of a pinhead, so small that it's hard to see.

Red oak acorns take two years to ripen. These photos show how they look at the end of their first summer and the middle of their second summer. In white oaks, acorns take only one year to ripen.

Each fall a red oak has one crop of ripe acorns. It also has a second crop that will be ripe the next fall.

Acorns and other nuts are food for many animals. Some, such as black bears, simply eat them. Others, such as blue jays and squirrels, eat some and lose some. They may carry away nuts and drop them. They may hide nuts and forget them. Many trees grow from nuts that animals drop, hide, or bury.

Travelers with the Wind

COLUMBINE

The wind spreads even more seeds than animals do.

Some flowers make tiny light seeds. These are like specks of dust that blow away on the wind. Some flowers make fruits with parachutes, which travel on the wind. Still other flowers make seeds that are shaken out of their fruits when the wind blows. Columbine is one of these.

You find columbine in gardens, and you also find it growing wild. Its flowers may be blue, white, red, or yellow.

As the fruits start to form, the petals of the flowers fall away.

A ripe fruit splits open along its seams. Now there are five pods. Each is packed with seeds.

The pods open into tubes. When the wind blows, the tall plant sways and bends. The seeds roll out of the tubes and are scattered.

POPPY

Other plants scatter their seeds in much the same way. Poppies, irises, snapdragons, and butter-and-eggs are four of them.

You can see the poppy fruit forming at the center of the petals. Soon the petals fall away and only the fruit is left. It is full of seeds.

The top of the fruit is a lid. When the seeds are ripe, the lid pushes up. There are little holes beneath it. When the wind blows, the poppy sways. The seeds are scattered through the holes, like salt from a shaker.

BULL THISTLE

Thistles, such as this one, are prickly. The stems, the leaves, and even the flowers have sharp prickles. Grasp a thistle and you'll think you have grabbed a handful of pins.

This plant is a bull thistle. It grows nearly everywhere.

The bull thistle has small pink-purple flowers that grow in flower heads. Each flower makes its own fruit and seed.

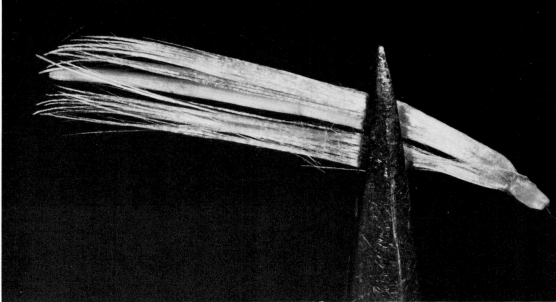

This photograph shows how the flower looks after the petals have fallen off. Inside it is packed with fruits and seeds and fine silky hairs.

Each fruit has its own group of hairs, which is called a pappus. This pappus and the fruit are being held by tweezers (upper right). The pappus is a clue to how the thistle fruit will travel.

When the fruits are ripe, the covering bursts. Pappuses spread out, becoming parachutes. Even a breath of wind will carry off the silky parachute and fruit.

25

Fruits with parachutes can travel far. A strong wind may carry them miles from the parent plant. A thistle fruit is held to its parachute by a collar (left). When the fruit lands, the parachute falls off. Now the seed may sprout and grow.

26

DANDELION

Everyone knows what a dandelion looks like. But most people don't know it belongs to the same family as the thistle. So does lettuce, and so does goldenrod. All of these plants have flower heads made up of many tiny flowers. The fruits of all these flowers fly away on parachutes.

Dandelion pappuses form a blow ball. At the end of each pappus is a fruit. Its tip fits into a little hole in the base of the flower head. Notice the barbs on the fruit. When the fruit lands, the barbs catch on the ground. The wind blows the pappus loose from the fruit.

These dandelion fruits are ripe and ready to travel. But the pappuses are closed up. What's wrong? It's a rainy day, and the silky parachutes can't work.

The weather changes, and the air becomes dry. The pappuses open wide and become parachutes that will carry off the fruits and seeds.

GOLDENROD

Goldenrod flowers form small fruits. This fruit and its parachute are hanging by a spider's thread from the parent plant. The fruit and its seed will float away on the first breeze.

MILKWEED

Milkweed blooms in summer, with clusters of pink or purple flowers.

The fruits are pods. In the beginning they are soft, green, and velvety. As time passes they become bigger and tougher and turn their tips toward the sky. The pods are lined with seams when ripe.

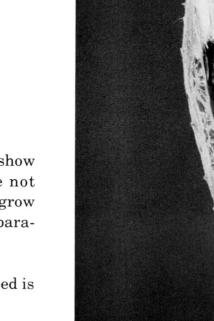

What's inside a pod? This one has been cut open to show you. More parachutes! But these parachutes are not attached to their fruits. The long white silky hairs grow from the seeds. Hundreds of brown seeds and their parachutes are packed inside each fruit.

These photos show you how a parachute opens. The seed is being held in place by a piece of clay.

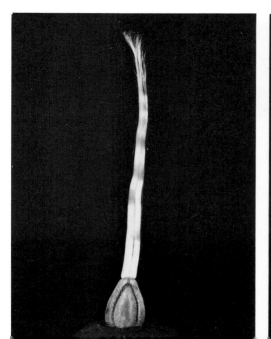

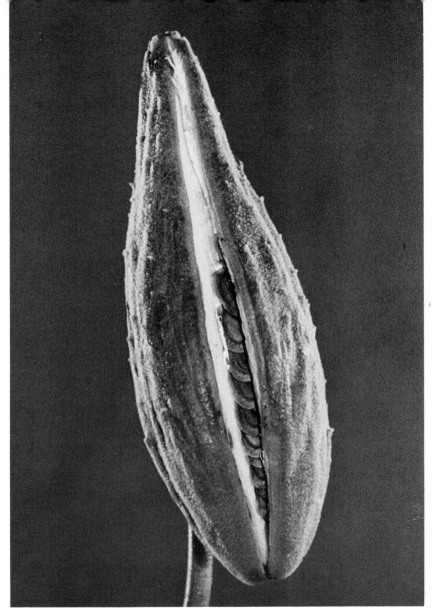

Each seed has about 900 silky hairs. The hairs are hollow and light. They are coated with wax, which keeps out water. Each seed also has a corky rim. It acts as a life preserver if the seed falls in water.

A ripe milkweed pod opens by splitting along a seam. When the wind comes along, it catches the parachutes and pulls them out of the pod.

NORWAY MAPLE

Like the oaks, maple trees have flowers, fruits, and seeds. The fruits are wing-shaped, and they grow in pairs.

By the time the fruits ripen, the seeds inside are big and heavy. The paired fruits turn down and split apart.

When the wind shakes it loose from a tree, the fruit spins round and round. The spinning slows its fall. It stays longer in the air and is carried farther by the wind. The seeds are so heavy that it takes a high wind to carry them very far.

When a seed sprouts, the fruit rots away. A new maple takes root. In this photo, part of the fruit has been cut away to show the seed inside.

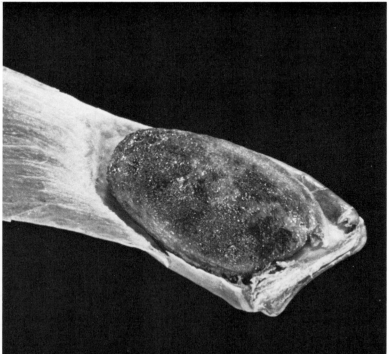

OTHER WINGED FRUITS

Seeds of several other trees also glide away on the wind. Watch for them and see how many you can find. Here are the big winged fruits of an ash tree,

the tiny winged fruit of an elm, being held between thumb and forefinger, and the large fruit of a linden, whose wing is formed by a bract.

RUSSIAN THISTLE

Russian thistle grows where the land is open and the air is dry. It blooms with tiny flowers. Their fruits are packed with seeds.

By the time the seeds are ready to travel, the plant has dried up. It breaks off near the ground and curls up.

When the wind catches it, the plant tumbles along the ground. That is why it is also called a tumbleweed. In a high wind it may bound along at speeds of up to 70 miles an hour. It sheds its fruits and seeds as it travels.

Travelers in Water

WATER LILY

Some seeds travel with animals, some with the wind. Still others travel with water.

During a heavy rain, water runs down hills and paths and along gutters. It picks up seeds and carries them away.

The water lily is a plant that grows in lakes and ponds. Its seeds float away in little cases of jelly. After a while the jelly melts. The seeds fall to the bottom, where they sprout and grow. Sometimes the seeds are eaten by fish. If they pass right through a fish, they may be dropped far from the parent plant.

Seeds of land plants may fall in streams and lakes. If they are light and corky, like milkweed seeds, they will float. Some of them reach places where they can sprout and grow.

COCONUT

Streams flow into rivers and rivers flow into the sea. They carry millions of seeds along with them. Most kinds die in salt water. Only a few can live in it and reach shore.

The most famous sea traveler is the coconut. Coconuts grow on coconut palm trees. They are found in tropical lands and islands.

Flowers keep blooming on a coconut palm all through the year. And so the fruits, or coconuts, keep forming all year long. Fruits take about twelve months to ripen.

The outside of a ripe coconut fruit is a waterproof coat. It keeps seawater out. Inside the coat is a husk made of fibers and air. It acts as a life preserver. Inside the husk is a hard shell. And inside the shell is the seed—the part you eat. It is one of the biggest seeds in the world.

If no one picks ripe coconuts, they fall to the ground and roll. Sometimes they roll into the sea and are carried away. High tides and waves may throw them ashore somewhere else.

On shore, rain, sand, and sun wear down the waterproof coat. Fresh water gets into the fruit, and the seed sprouts.

Travelers that Scatter Themselves

VIOLET

Some plants don't need animals, wind, or water to spread their seeds. They scatter their own seeds. The violet is one of these plants, and what happens may surprise you.

In the spring, violets bloom in fields and gardens and on the edge of woods. People often pick the flowers, but this does not stop the violet plants from making seeds.

In late spring the plants make other flowers. These flowers are hard to see. They have no petals and they are hidden under the leaves. This is what one looks like.

The fruit of a hidden flower ripens all summer. Then the stem stiffens and pulls the fruit up from the ground. In this photo, the leaves have been tied back to show what happens.

A few inches above the ground, the fruit splits open. It has three parts that turn outward. Each looks like a tiny canoe filled with seeds.

As a canoe dries, it shrinks. Its sides bend and press together, squeezing the seeds. One by one, the seeds pop out, just the way a melon seed pops when you squeeze it between your fingers. A violet seed can travel several feet from the parent plant.

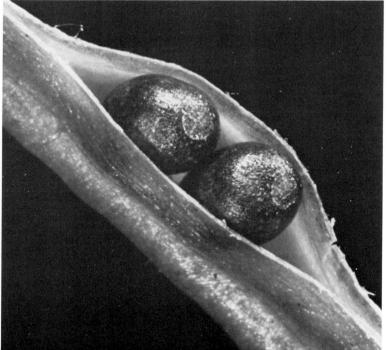

WITCH HAZEL

Witch hazel is another plant that pops its seeds. This tree grows on the edge of woods and forests, and it blooms in late fall. When other trees have shed their leaves, witch hazel opens its yellow flowers. The fruits ripen during the following summer and early fall.

The fruit is a pod that holds two large shiny black seeds. When the seeds are ripe, the pod opens (below left).

Dry air moves through the pod. It shrinks and presses on the seeds, and out they pop!

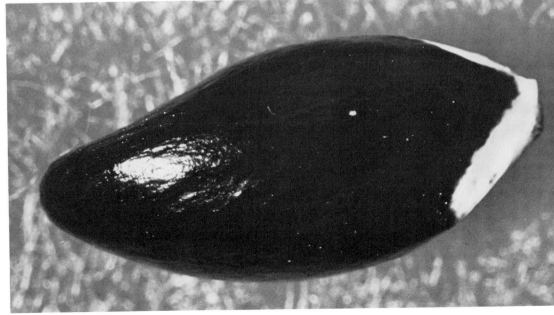

WOOD SORREL

Common wood sorrel is a small plant with a tiny yellow flower. Like the clovers, it folds its leaves as night draws near and opens them again toward dawn.

Its fruits are pods, with slits in them. You can see the seeds inside this pod.

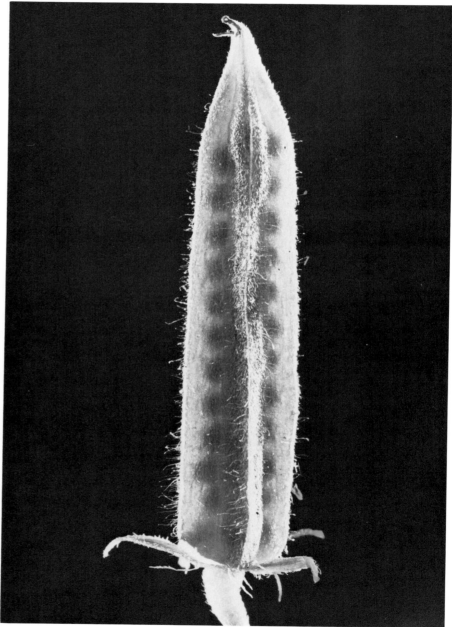

Each seed has a thin hard outer coat. Inside this is a thick soft coat.

About the time the seeds are ripe, the inner coat takes in water and swells. The outer coat loses water and shrinks. Something is bound to snap—and it does. The outer coat bursts. The inner coat springs back and tosses the seed out through the slit.

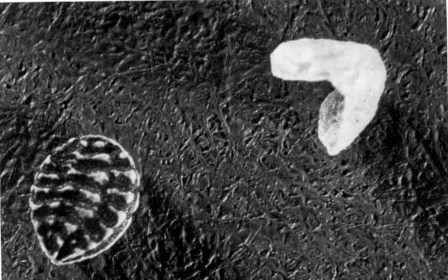

TOUCH-ME-NOT

The touch-me-not is a small plant that grows in damp woodsy places. It blooms in late summer with speckled orange or yellow flowers. Another name for it is jewelweed.

Each flower forms a fruit that is a pod. The pod is made up of strap-shaped pieces that fit together. Each strap is like a spring that has been stretched. When it later lets go, it swiftly coils up.

As the seeds ripen and become bigger, the pod grows longer. The straps are stretched more and more. When the seeds are fully ripe, the straps have stretched as far as they can go. The slightest touch makes the pod explode.

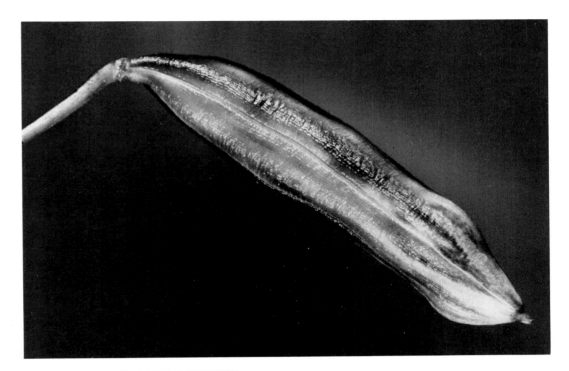

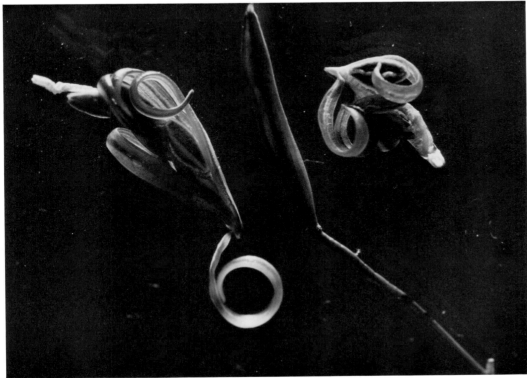

The energy of the coiling straps carries pods off. They sail through the air, scattering seeds as they go.

WILD OAT

Some fruits and seeds have ways of creeping away from the parent plant. The wild oat is one of these. It is shaped like a wedge, with barbs and a long tail.

Changes in moisture make the oat move. During the day, the amount of moisture in the air changes. When the air is damp, the oat takes up moisture. The tail circles slowly clockwise. When the air is dry, the oat loses

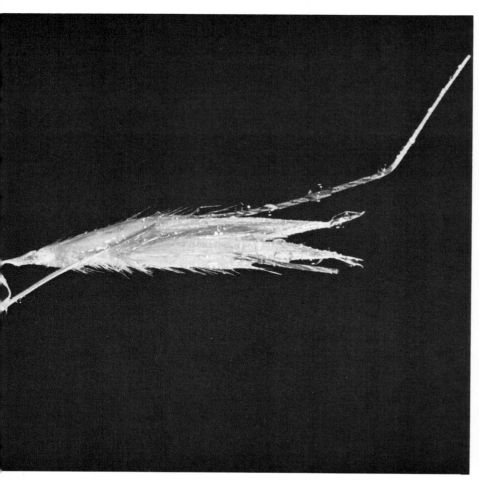

moisture. The tail circles slowly counterclockwise. The tail also moves slowly up and down.

The moving tail drives the wedge forward and the barbs keep it from moving backward or sideways. The oat does not move very far or very fast. But it does move away from the parent plant. Finally, the tail drives the oat into soft ground—and the oat is planted.

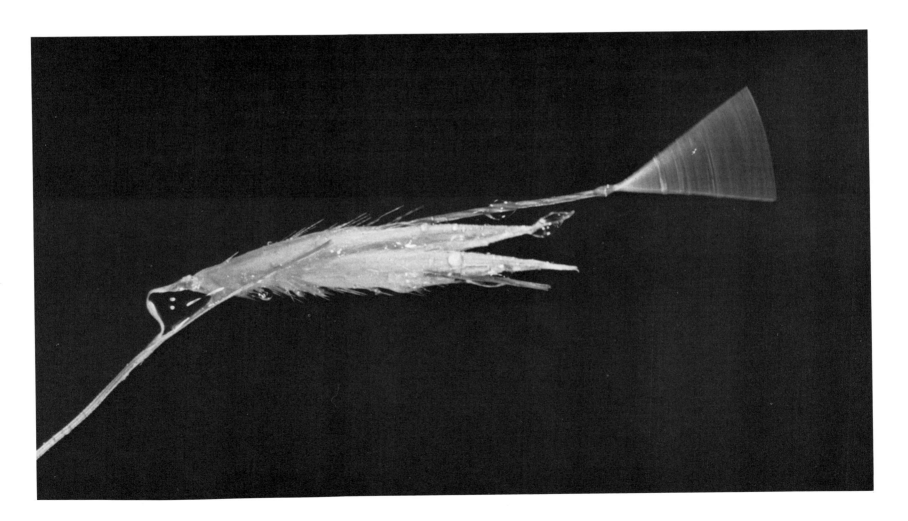

What Seeds Are

Some creep. Some pop. Some float. Some glide. Some travel with people and animals. Whatever they do, billions and billions of seeds are on the move every year. Of them all, only some arrive in places where they can grow. There, at the right time, they will sprout. They will grow into new flowering plants and make seeds of their own.

Seeds are made by the male and female parts of flowers. Two things are needed to make a seed.

One is an egg cell. Egg cells form in the female parts of plants. They look like tiny seeds, but they are not. If you planted them, they would not grow. Egg cells are seeds-to-be.

The second is the contents of a grain of pollen from the same kind of plant. Pollen forms in the male parts of flowers.

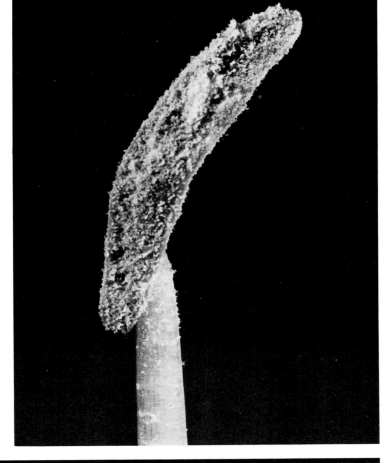

Masses of pollen grains have formed at the center of the daffodil. The grains are like sticky specks of dust. The close-up photo shows a mass of these grains.

When the contents of a pollen grain join an egg cell, the egg is fertilized. It is on its way to becoming a seed. The photos below show you part of what happens.

The egg cells of this daffodil have been fertilized. As time passes, the base of the flower starts to swell and grow. This is the part of the flower that becomes the fruit.

Inside it, seeds have started to ripen.
More time passes. When the seeds are fully
ripe the fruit opens and the seeds spill out.

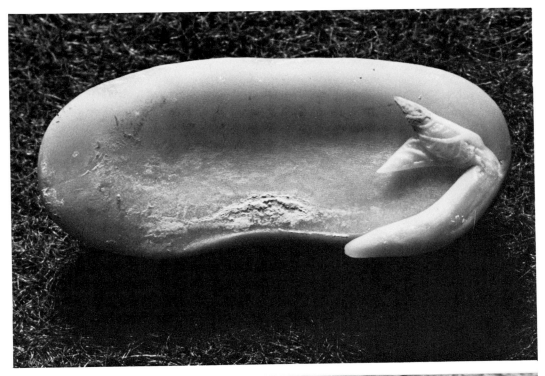

What is a seed? It is a package of life. Every seed holds a tiny living plant. Most kinds also hold a supply of food. The tiny plant uses this food until it can make its own. The plant and its food are packed inside a seed coat.

You can see this for yourself with a big seed. Take a seed from a string bean or a lima bean. Soak it in water overnight. The next day, gently split it open. Look at what's inside.

There's a tiny plant, with leaves. Around it is part of the food supply. The other half of the seed holds still more food.

When a seed is ripe, it stops growing. The life inside seems to stop. It is as if the little plant had gone to sleep. A long time may pass. Nothing happens. Then one day—in the right place at the right time—the seed starts to sprout.

53

First a root grows out of the seed.
It anchors itself in the soil.

A stalk appears and stiffens. It grows up,
toward the light, and the leaves appear.

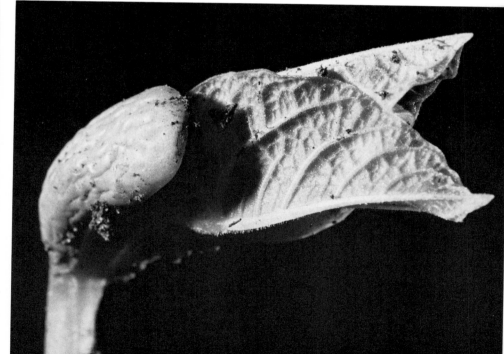

As you can see, the seed's food supply is used up now, but that's all right. The young plant has leaves. Like all green plants, it makes its own food in its leaves.

The young plant grows and grows. Soon it puts out flowers. It has taken the first step toward making its own seeds.

This book has shown you only a few of the many kinds of seeds in the world. You can discover many more by being a good observer outdoors.

Choose three or four flowering plants in spring. Go look at them often and watch what happens as petals fade and fruits form. (A hand lens will be a help.) Try to find out what happens to the seeds.

In late summer and fall look for other seeds. What is the wind carrying? Can you find some afloat? What's sticking to your clothes? What animals are eating fruits and seeds? Look for small animals as well as big ones. You may even find ants carrying off seeds.

You'll be surprised at how much is going on around you, once you know what to look for.

Index